BEDLAM'S BEST & FINEST

BEDLAM'S BEST & FINEST

MICHAEL WILSON

POETRY

 EYEWEAR PUBLISHING

First published in 2018
by Eyewear Publishing Ltd
Suite 333, 19-21 Crawford Street
Marylebone, London W1H 1PJ
United Kingdom

Cover design and typeset by Edwin Smet
Cover photograph by Melvin Abdon Flores Yames
Author photograph by Andy O'Hara
Printed in England by TJ International Ltd, Padstow, Cornwall

ISBN 978-1-912477-26-5

WWW.EYEWEARPUBLISHING.COM

Dedicated to my brothers John and Pog

Michael Wilson
studied at the universities of Warwick
and Manchester, specialising in postmodern American
Literature, Film and Media. Over the years, he
established himself as part of the vibrant Manchester
poetry scene. After winning the 2010 Cheltenham
Festival UK All Stars Slam, he began touring parts
of the UK. His street art took him around some of
England's biggest cities. He also reached the final of
the BBC Radio 4 Slam (2009). His pamphlet *After All
Tomorrow's After Parties* (2010) is published by Knives,
Forks and Spoons Press. He is currently part of a
conduit group serving families of addicts and
lives in Northern Ireland.

TABLE OF CONTENTS

PREFACE

There is no real beginning to this story. There's a potted history of my illness I have to recite every time I meet a medical professional for the first time. That history is about as concise as a gravestone and just as telling.

In reality, the last twenty years have been anything but concise, potted or straightforward. They have been a forced invitation to the strangest of curiosities, an ushering into a live debate on the romanticising of mental illness, its many taboos, myths and urban legends. Mental illness makes all its sufferers experts.

There is one element, a key element, that I neglect to mention to the medical professionals, and that is my ongoing attempts, whenever ill, to try and solve life's big questions. This book has two threads throughout: hope and learning. Hope that no matter how terrible things get, things will get better, that even in the death of things, light finds a way through. Second to this, learning is a belief at times that the mysteries of life are not only knowable, but ultimately changeable. What I am left with is a sense of responsibility, privilege, danger, but most of all love of the world and all those I care for. This book is a faithful explanation of that drive to understand, and a wish to change the world.

As for the history of my treatment, that is detailed in the following pages from hospital into psychosis, wellness and care in the community, as well as panic attacks and midnight flits to other countries and cities; life is rarely boring.

Michael Wilson, July 2018

FOREWORD

Fallowfield, Manchester used to have an open mic night in a bar called Trof, where you could hear music, poetry, even comedy sometimes. It was a weird mixture that could pitch a beat-boxer next to a poet, followed by a singer-songwriter; it sometimes involved improvised collaborations (I read a poem once to an improvised trumpet, as did Michael). Both Michael and I honed our performance skills in this event, and it was a brilliant forum for trying things out and experimenting. Michael struck me from the time I met him as someone keen to explore the edges of performance poetry and to move beyond what was expected.

Experimenting with performance and writing is at the heart of Michael's writing, alongside an often searing emotional honesty about the history of his own mental health. The way his poems sometimes break up their form and language at times reflects the course of his illness and recovery; it's not simply there to be clever or 'avant garde', though some of the techniques he uses may have originated in that world. Here, the fragmentary nature of the narrative reflects the fragmenting personality of the ill mind.

There's plenty of comedy here too, and in the end, hope of recovery. This is not a simplistic 'misery memoir'; there's an honesty and a depth to the writing that doesn't flinch from the reality of his situation: his use of alcohol and drugs as self-medication for instance. But there's also beauty and love and help along the way, and in the end, light breaks through the darkness.

The language is honed and sharp; but there's also a flamboyance about it, a joy in words as play, that lift this long poem above the general run of poetry. He cares for the sound; there's a milder Dylan Thomas in these lines. The experiments with form are not simply reflective of a state of mind he's trying to explain; when he scatters words about the page like a constellation, he's doing so because it makes a visual and oral shape that looks and sounds great.

When I saw him perform from this book recently, I was struck by the quiet energy of his voice. Those soft Northern Irish vowels and consonants were not shouted out; he sat down to recite as if he were a storyteller, as if he were talking to the audience one-to-one. You sometimes had to strain to hear, because he was making you listen. I was struck all the time by the images and sounds, moving together musically. His quietness, to quote Frank O'Hara, has a man in it: a good man.

Michael has had a hard life, but that would not in itself make for great poetry. What makes it great, and memorable, is the sheer control and love of language revealed throughout this collection. It requires reading aloud, quietly, to yourself.

Steven Waling

BEDLAM'S BEST & FINEST

there are many ways in
there are always white sheets

i knew this because i had been there
so many times –
countless really, seven really
when my numb fingers could count

lay the body down
stare at the face written into the pillow

it all started in October
out of everywhere

1. *a blessing*

bless the world
not to feel this

i felt if i wrote these words
i felt if i tried to describe
the   broken   mess   of   self
somehow the illness would transfer
like those old grazes we had as kids:
give me your arm, apply water, apply pressure
lift and find
but temporary
a smudge of colour bright

2. *shattered*

the mind lies / like broken glass / it's a different version / – *sugar*

took a call / cooked some eggs / with chilli flakes / seemed to be what he'd want / – *salt*

video on pause / the figurine in the window / reflection / we were all stuck in rooms / they spoke to me earlier / in that breathless / pin of a place / the body language / mind bending / – *pepper*

parents tried to ease me onto white sheets / butchery / i could see them like that Dali painting / which? / *Autumnal Cannibalism* / they didn't know / heard whistles from the chimney / bird-like / men with guns / – *play*

shudder of darkness / raised my foot over the lip of the sofa / left foot / religion / all the trade-words of the body /

earlier he said *you're going on an adventure* / a gap / failing / cold laughter / – *ha*

sugar: the inescapable. *salt*: the choice you made, will make. *pepper*: control. *play*: punishment for knowledge. forbidden. *ha*: the inability to measure pain

3. disintegration

character stuck in bedsit, stuck with self, suffering little fuck

smoke – though your eyes roll upwards – smoke – though it's destroying you – those hands don't even shake – but your core does –

earlier those lights looked pretty, didn't they?
there was a horrible feeling juddering through you
no gap between you and the world
breathing in over and over

(the bus screamed in your head
all those people)

as you fell through your eyes
you can't even tell yourself how it feels

character walks back and forth, character tries to watch tv, forever pained by something the eye can't see but which is noticeable through his body language

so smoke – another – and another – all you can do – that and clutch that alarm clock – in hands that don't know why – suffer –

A
R
H
G
Gjfldjs
thought after
thought
thought

                    thought
thhoughtttt
         feel
UPPPP
/////ggg///g///gg//gg/g///ggg///gg///g//////////
all lufe ends wath a fall stoppp. why does?
wash i could ecplaine how thede fellll
nos. no no no 3422899
repeat
repeat
repeat
the sense of panikkkkkk thought becomes feeling becomes feeling becomes thought
becomenes thought befrmend s thought dnejwjsm feeling djdmKA gleffess is language
sense? Gerrettttteeeee.

4. dissociation

i can see her frustration. we've had these sessions so many times now. nothing works, but still i show up and she runs through a few techniques. they're too strong, way too strong. i feel like both of us are just entertaining each other.
(i watch the staff clean up the floor, the tiled chipped floor, and think about how it feels)

distraction

distraction

distraction

self

avoid

distraction

distraction

dissent

of

self
home dry and safe is butter sweet

sting

shock

stars
lights   broken

asked

hide

doors

bus

inevitability

of

constellations
even the bed gets bitten into

ah well, home soon.
my partner's hand on my shoulder holds little in it, not his fault, mine. his hand on my shoulder leaves a tattoo.

5. *nights on Allsorts*

the windows watch | the accursed flat | look down over like masters | over poor Scruffy | Scruffy
feels wrong done to | it's no one's concern | but the windows look down | with no one else to
watch | they watch the nothing going on | except the rattle in his head | of all the things he
worries about |

        he isn't for you

                he's an empty crisp packet of a person these days

                    he's been here before and he'll be here many times after

                          suffering fuck

Scruffy sits in a slump of a sofa   half in and half out

                                          it's no way to be

now, we can do this one of two ways
you can pay me to watch him
or you can just pretend you're passing through
just rubbernecking
it's all charity
it helps him
he needs something like this

suffering Scruffy | nights have been low here | business never so good | it's high time he felt the
grind of days the grind of days the grind of days the grind of days   the grind of   days
the grind   ofdays the   grindofdays   the   grind   of   days   the grind
of days the grind of days the   g   r   i   n
d
of   days   the
grind of   days the grind the grind the grind of
                            days
ha! i knew you'd flinch.

blessed Scruffy, this is what you get for those nights on *Allsorts*, thinking like this, but it ran like honey, now it chips like teeth

                              like zipper mouth
                                   like chipped needle
you smoked your way through your twenties
you   took   too much   fool you
      mixedup   all   your   thuoghts
like   selfish   dull   you
            lederickranmynamedforthesakeofjesus
                  fool   you   Scruff
so we watch   and we watch   and we watch
      and you sit there and know – as the sun runs a smear through the sky
                        crosses flash in the night

++

      run like lightening in your head poor poor poooooor Scruff suffering fuck

                                          you've got green eyes, you know
                                             just in there, a hint of green
                                             for all the things you can't do

don't pity
take heart
you'll get through like we all do
there is laughter at the end of everything

6. a spoonful of sugar

remember when she brought you your pills you'd jumped clean
through a window onto the grass you remember and they were so
glad you took your meds but you were still sure they were going
to kill you but you thought well you've done all you can what is is
besides maybe you're wrong and you took them in that dark metallic
room with the figures sleeping and their snoring voices sounded like
a language and you thought they were talking to each other plotting
great plots for plots underneath the steady snores like waters and you
lifted the plastic cup and there was a large hole in the base and water
ran out and you said *there's a hole in my bucket, dear Liza* you could hear
the nurse's smile inside the black – always go out with a joke

7. some thoughts on wellness

wellness runs
like well
wellness runs like a salted treat, it reminds me of how bad things are but there's the rub.

illness brings pain, wellness brings further change: the lessons learned, broken over the back, exist to live like a scaled down candle that can burn in all weathers, for a time, but medication is the drug of the masses – ha – it runs through me, and there's a resistance to it; days   drop off   and it runs like a slug through me when i try and take it again.

8. Hope's spittle

hospital
Hope's spittle

i can take it from you   *i'm the devil i'm the devil*

                          shut up you aren't

i replied, in the cannibal waiting bays, in the same accent. i can't remember the words, but
the tone was *don't think you can get to me that easily…*
the first night i was taken to the old green-rust-copper-topped hospital, the nurses stayed
up with me as i sat in an armchair, on top of the white sheet they'd bury me in, and every
trip to the toilet escorted of course.
there was a man in a bed, made of sweat, clawing the air, and cigarette burns around the
old-style baths, the tiles, the chipped tiles, and my dark eyes in the mirrors.
the next day i asked what the treatment would be like. it took them a while to work out
what to do with me because i appeared to know things.

then,
i woke and found myself in hospital
                    so i danced into the main room
                              whisper singing
                                        please release me

thinking at worst
they might find me funny
the young man there took me as a cue
and finally took his tablet
one box ticked
always go out with a joke

i woke and found my brain
    was sliced in two   and stitchted back together sloppsily

 the music on the radio was them about losing a war fought – a war fraught
     but i saw just the shaking hand that held that pill
     melting they said
     in my hand
           days felt listless then
       moving from terror to calmness to boredom
    and back
  like songs on repeat
or tracks on a damaged cd or candy floss stuck in the grinder or hands trampled by horses hands
high – hand high

i had never felt such fear
and i had already seen myself the devil
do unspeakable acts
all too cold
and as my body shook in the last bed
i knew death was a light

there was humour here
the man slicked with sweat
with an orange string bag full of fuck-off oranges
he threw them, all muscular and angry, at the staff –
     who temporarily lost that quivering control
       and ducked this way, hither and thither
      while rock hard oranges came flying
     backed into a corner, holding court
    he battled them off until the ammo ran dry
got one though, the student nurse
nice guy, keen
got in too close, got a broken nose
he spent time in the cooler for that

one was a runner: a week or two from getting out
he hitched a lift halfway across Northern Ireland
first night with the medication bleeding out
i spoke with him to strike up a conversation
a kind of common sense running though the confusion of here
i thought he was here to kill me
i thought it best to talk
change minds that can be changed

thought comes from somewhere
the mind full of days spent under the sheets
like a kid in a useless fort
playtime with the nurses
playing catch with tube socks
rubbed into a ball

he seemed nice
he ran up walls
anchored and pulling at the chaff rope in the cd room
said he was here for shouting on Christmas Day
pulled out a joke that dinner about Christmas
(someone ran out
you couldn't make jokes here
and walking into rooms was hard)
he told me he was an actor
wanted me to act in a film
without a camera
wanted a reshoot

i didn't know what to do

apparently i walked in trances   made others shifty
    i did not make friends there   made me less of someone

but i had read *The Prince* before the harshness   ploughed in
knew always to play your hand   or perhaps it didn't matter

those days had the taste of too many cigarettes   ash

9. dream versus reality or when the road turns into a river

i wish they'd never told me

but i'm glad i can see the world as it is
can dreadnought

you see they were right
all those conspiracy-violent-green minded
lost in their metal cubes

i am outside, can use it on the field, all knowledge: to know, the action of knowing is worth a
million words, each step a test

Manchester runs white   a grip test in white January   dark rain sizzles the traffic
neon of curry mile   dark gaps between Fallowfield   and there and here
like gaps between   worlds   and countries

                                                          (what is the book?
                                                           what is the ring?
                                                     is it a coin or a sound?)

                                            (a call, must find that one open door
                                         every car registration plate there as a marker
                                              like orientation, childhood games
                                               children love the grotesque)

Sleep is anaemic
she wouldn't understand

                                                    the city skyline

                        the stacked flats
                                              of houses

and women's heels

                                                          alright choose
yes
              no

                                        binary choices
like Pynchon

                  like Frost

                              like Joyce

                                          like Tolkien

nightmoves, knightmoves, nitemovies, everything is play, stops and starts, flows and backwash:
the road turns into a river: this will be a stay in my life for years: at that junction it was bubbles
  of air round breaking traffic in rows: like a movie part played – all is movie, choice and where
  life goes: this is the lunch hour: the opposite side of the clock at 1am is 1pm-2pm, that means
  essay in at 2am, if 2 is inverted (ha, that makes sense): the place behind the day, the night, isn't
    the opposite it's the partner of day, the two hold hands twice a day, but the sun is away, like a
  vacant landholder: this is the lunch hour, where all has to be delivered, like a letter (i will learn
  later that Joyce hinted or wrote the same, but in a different book): the night: we all contain the
                                            same dream, it runs like this

/
    move
        ∧
          event
             ★
               act
                  (reaction)
                     next move
                        ><

each time there are marks, but the answer will come when i make it to the open door, scaled down in the mind, a scaled-up version of university corridors: i find her office, always turn left, follow people who look suspicious, read meaning into letters of signs
e.g.: casino = sin

casino	smoke comes	from door	street empty
part people	no one in	no one out	follow names
follow fate	didn't believe before	iron clad sure	clinking armour
green coat	led to bridge	led under bridge	song
says	die	every choice	slips finger

cold snap | frostbitten yellow piss pavements | but there is hope here | somewhere in these moments | just stay away from the devil | though hell is hollow | just a made-up façade | a listening device | say nothing | snap

10. *photograph 51*

certain albums romance me certain
albums hurt because they sing of loss
the world is birthed to music born of
the air certain albums mean they were
written for all of us when we leap into
the black into the white and the grey

do you want to ride with us?
he looks fucked
sober part of the brain
says *no*

cruel summer   lie here   he
                                        suggests

          backstory   they are   many have
                             filming   seen

what i did   unlocking   the gates
before   open the
now   figurines
                                       angry and
                                       tense

          spill onto   i have   i am out
          the streets   missed
                              time

i walk   shimmering   nights out
home   lights out

turn from   turn in   coat left
yellow   your skin   in road

no island   just torrent   car
there   waters   stopped

lights   puked   sense all
door open   the world

throwing   purging   all i do is
spit

i am Miller   i am Kazan   the lunch
hour is
over what
you learn?

nothing   no thing   i am
nothing
but lost

i cannot go   i must let   the pain of
back   no one   a silenced
know   tongue

burns   she must   adult life
like flame   not know   with all its
power

the promise   is lost to
we were   the young
given as
kids

for weeks they drove me home a different road. i was too bashful to tell them. i took both and the one they drove me home along was the second one, known only to myself.

11. all that glitters

it takes
forever to
take away the
pain of a low

and sense it's
joy

    it takes
    forever and
    ever to lose
    the thrill of a
    high

and sense is
numbered

    serial said
    words won't
    let you fly

sometimes
when a
certain song
plays

    i feel the
    open canyon
    of a high

i have learned
to step back

it was not always this way

so?   so?

i danced so
blissskill

    watched
    and
    listened
    and saw

and saw
and saw
see

    back and
    forth

there must be payment

but it frees so it must be   ok   ok

i'm ok   i'm ok

to see the shimmer of   on a train back from   i can feel

happiness   Amsterdam

it fires through my   like cyber cyphers

head   of delicious information

you found it   you walked through   you visited each

blameless this time   realm

you walked over the   walked the ice ponds of

thin snow of January   the winter park

crossed it's basin black   the lights like a bay   felt the wind of

the night before   cold comfort

the ice burn of hell   the joy of conversation

over black coffee teeth

the demons all closed in   passed the joint to no one but   like spilling blood

on the smoking denizen   myself   to arise a demon

and finding a way out of   these mazes of streets

they said they know the   leave them to boast   know it all

end of it all   half dead brains

12. tulips from Amsterdam

there is joy in these thoughts...
like the girl who dressed to stay warm, except her hands were cold. i gave her mine. she rolled
a cigarette and ate the cold visible air. we chattered teeth over the subject of the Tudors and she
showed me art and got me a free ticket to Hoek. she got me out of black-wind Rotterdam, the ice
breath of some god or other flooding through the doors. we laughed instead at the cold.
i may be a fool to these experiences but, to be honest, they work well when you meet and my
strangeness doesn't come across.
like that woman. i asked if she was ok. the grin on her face made me shine, just light up a little, and
i stepped off hell into a new realm.

                       the tower clock
                       of Amsterdam

       i kept coming   a starting block
       across

       like a leash   on a dog

       turning the   round and
       same way   round the
                                   pencil streets
                   ragged tyke

once the room	the books	the whole place	and the place
became a feather	moved a little	jiggled	changed itself like
			weather
there were faces	looking out	cartoonish figures	she said i was
in her wardrobe	impassively	in the hall	doing so well

just let it happen

the fan sounded
like a dj i know of

commenting
about music it
liked

we used to watch
the strangest tv

one time the train
sounded like the
end of all music

the kettle roar of
the kitchen

the people in the
lounge through
the window

dissolved with the
open door

there is only one
entrance with
these things

and one way
throughout

choice is a
blessing

to the skin-wrap
minded

love like

love like snow

newspaper flakes

13. someone to watch over me

i spent nights alive with my own company
and brass bands
and songs whose videos looked like keynotes
keystones

there is a
fumble to
God

He is
messy in
what He
does

and
heaven is
lithe

i know this
because so
is my mind

like great
blooms

of the
head

the pot
plant alive
and
writhing

i am every
film hero
likewise

all my
friends like
others there

at nights i
come
home

half
expecting
them to be
arranged

like pieces
of
furniture

divided
one by one

but all
there to
say

in and out
of breath

they are
my friend
to the last

but in the room there is only one
myself
but they watch and watch and watch and watch
i do not mind
i look and listen
to the great rivers and lakes coming through the tv

there is magic
in the pupils

you can see it   the love
glimmer there

the messages   they know
                                                            who knows
                                                            who looks
                                                            back

and sees a   stone   gold   and diamond   that cries
note hastily   formed   silent
written

tears of great
joy

but also of loss

for those who
never made it
back again

like a friend i
lost, what did
he see?

before he fell

polymaths

14. synchronicity

they told me i was special
that i was what one day i would find meant
gifted
i thought it was a curse
there is no epiphany

i change my mood about this as regularly
as i'm able to envision
able to be sensitive
to change this world
like a hero

and now like our Lord
we play out an analogy
over the Last Supper

walk the day
under the shadows of birds high
seeing the regular synch of life; it's all
meant to be it's all so obvious and there
for anyone who takes a moment to search
and once seen and felt and most of all
believed there is no way back; each
time was a deadened end
but this time
this time
time

i saw my grandparents the past night
they appeared at the graveyard

like comic characters
just there to say
ok son of ours
which way is it to be?

but i will not swim the ocean
i have barely eaten
it would do me no good

part of me takes play
like an inner parent
you can enjoy but be careful
and tell no one
you cannot know who keeps
a shared secret
the whole world shares

i have discovered how the mechanics tuned us
like the idea of *click – start – stop – go – move forward – and back again*
there is sync in everything

like the day
i woke without sleeping first, woke
like Christmas Day when i was a wee thing, got up
from the bed and walked, still dark, out to the beach – timed
excelsior, the rise of the sun. i saw one folk out in the black, we
said our hellos, he was returning, me setting out for the other edge;
maybe there i was watched over, though everyone takes the walk
alone. white light was alive at the Barmouth, and i clambered
over the rocks to its shelf, sat there, then walked along
to the place where the Bann and the
ocean hold hands.

i drew a stick from my pocket deep – broke it –
and at the apex threw one and one
to give *thanks, much precious, appreciated to say*
i know what you give me
i had to sink on my knees and crawl forward
                              to the very fall
                                   to make sure one end made it
                                        with nothing left behind
                    i walked home wondering
                had i done the right thing?
           the colour of people's clothes
       the sense of warmth that answered

i remember

the pavement bank   we sea a-part as flashes   easy how things
                                                             churn out

a call   *you missed a bit*   they know you no

just   polymaths   pointing at the
                                                             coat
reached
           dreamtime   there are mechanics

15. Faustus

kneel
who is on the right side
God or the cursed twin?
Jesus spoke through animal

i sold myself cheap, too late
the phone said (recorded message):
we now possess your soul
tricked
and sold to men with all kinds of ways
to keep alive people whom they wish dead

blood red words

Nature is a power and if you go wrong you learn, and if you aren't supposed to (to the un-initiated) you can't stop it. it is the synchronicity of the world.

Nature is the fifth side of the die, one of two you can never see from any angle.

you played yourself into that game you knew
what you thought was 'living'
is only done by the old

i cursed my whole line
back and forth
and they will hang like stones
great mill wheels around my neck:
be good, if you can't be good, be careful,
if you can't be careful, get wed

advice with a different tong
maybe if i swallow the rite
i could curse myself but let my family go

16. make and do

choice is a bitter tong trap
there to trick the user
into thinking there's an ending in sight,
and the moment of life is just a blind blink
before the static dream of tortured infinite bale
the pitch and toss of life's game;
there's nothing to be won in betting early
and waking something that's there to be left alone

i'm talking to the whole of Ireland, i can tell
(amidst psychosis)
because of the colour of the nurse's green fleece

broadcast to the world the secret
you are nothing, you sold it
for nothing
then they can come
and destroy you for selling your soul.
it wouldn't save the world for knowing that's the trick
but i must know, will those i know be ok?

as i draw a circle and a dragon and anything else that comes to mind
like a troubled child shivering down through himself
because i've lost all language
nothing will help
only make the twist longer
and longer
of a cord that snaps the neck
snap

17. superman

there is no way to be a hero
it's just a hide
it feels like the suicidal are the brave ones:
now nothing makes me search that option
too much interference
i lost that way
i lost my family several times
don't
but at times
not to, is the saddest thing
a soul feels like it can do
and the inability
the very fail in my blood
running like an insult in my body
is hate in itself
still i remember

18. *helix*

stuck
animal realm
don't mind
strange
strained head
given up

they mop my leg
blood
to show
trick
of terrorists

dream-like
i let them
as they laugh
in the next room
x-ray
no break

another
time

too much
bother

cannibal
hospital

you see it

churns
and
clanks

in their
begrudging
professionalism

and fire

slice us up

they say

slice by
slice

trick

for the
cooker

it's the
furnace

no one knows

it's us

too many
lucid
conversations

all these
bays

no point
screaming

people
can't
move

just let it be

move
makes
worse

just no one else

i eat
breakfast

trust

they
don't
trust me

no one

19. don't break the fourth wall

but even here there is hope. it's in my oddest behaviour, to keep them guessing.

i showed staff the fingerspell alphabet. they might have entertained a fool, but every chance goes awry.

don't give up

keep mind

don't break the fourth wall

last night one questioned me, her hand fingers flickering in the corner of my eye, certainly trying to hypnotise me, certain certain certainly.

it's a fix one said, warning.

maybe he's ok.

maybe they know i know i know i know i know i know i know this is all flimsy backed paper these walls soaked of sense these places are infinite and if i had a way of looking at it i would say that they don't want this but someone has to do it. *ha. sugar. salt. pepper. ha.*

there's this thing called the game and it takes place on the streets. every so often blood has to be let, there must be balance and since i didn't leave town in time, i have now to stay and tell no one. i will be some kind of tramp with no way to live and if anyone talks i will just open my mouth and not say a word. there's humour in this and a dry kind of laugh heaved in my soul, something turned in my stomach. it's a Beckettian kind of humour, that all we do is trap ourselves, and as my thoughts dance over one another i see a light, that although i'm fucked there's a sense to it. just don't open the door.

20. poetry night

i once ran an event thinking gangs were after me for stopping taking drugs. so there's me, lost in my own bravery, in a place where the mood is low light and soft and people are reading and playing music and everyone is having a good time and there's someone i know who will be in the audience and i clock him, a working-class lad, at the back listening away and i read a poem about being at a rave, and i'm charmed and charming. earlier i'd asked the staff where the keys were, quoting a lyric from Tori Amos' 'Cornflake Girl' because you know, hero and all that, and i read this poem at the end and this youth turns up at me and says *that poem you did was great. i know what you mean, i get that from Acid* and he taps his head. *it does that for me, you ever need any let me know and i'll sort you out.* i told him no need but graciously took the compliment. it takes all sorts to make an episode. they realised that with *Friends*.

i mean it's funny when you think it out.

as if the world waits for me.

21. breathe in breathe out

i love you
is the cheesiest line
it's a pity it's said too much
it's beautiful said a little less
especially these days but to
me both are heavier than
the feather they use
to judge
this world
and this
world can damage
the eyes if looked at
for too long just know you're
both these things because the
opposite well it's there but
i'd rather not if you
don't mind

my poet friend said, *we were just talking about meditation and we end up talking about this.*
it left me wondering that eternal thought: do we all think the same?
like that childish idea: do we dream the same?

now and again
there are things you can know
laid out like a blanket

on the other side of thought
on the back of the map is written:
inside is a family
the little child, the older, the mother, the father

maybe these experiences are there
to tap into each one

maybe what causes closedness
is the inability to see the whole:
the back of the map
is a chart of frozen climes
the back of the map is the desert
both blank until you raise the thought of a pen —
maybe none of us is ever really alone

22. another thought on wellness

wellness
is a fear at times
but so is anything looked
at too long my thoughts aren't deeper
they're just the wrong way around they keep me
warm between winters and dark summers wellness
is an
armour

later, he walked through London with friends, face down, until he heard a song he couldn't deny and said *it's on in here*. he chose and sat down, Hero of the Late Hour.

wellness is an armour.

23. Nevermore

this town is called Nevermore
a beauty to itself
it's where i come to shire my head
it's where i came
when i found myself sitting alone

the flat i left had rats
damp tattooing the bottom of its legs

not caring any more
but here is Nevermore
it's where people come to speak
to each other on street corners
dancing in club not clubs

it has appeal in the multi-coloured ocean
it always says what it means
i will sing a song of songs for Nevermore
the sun explodes at night there
it has caught me when i've fallen

it did the same for a film maker, lost to the last string of flops and every good deed she ever did.
the town changed beauty into the beauty of coloured skies and caring feral dogs. she learnt
that she had to walk the beach, and she dreamt of a clearing at a festival she'd never been to,
and talked to the male version of herself. but direct questions can't be asked. the second law
of thermodynamics. she'd read it in a paperback – and all books become paperbacks, even the
classics.
i met her once, over a drink that clinked itself every time you picked it up. about her
strangeness... thoughts can be misleading. but i guess you'll never meet her, and she wants it that
way.

you meet all sorts in illness and recovery, recovery and wellness. we can open up others with a mere switch of the tongue. we can bring calm through our own weathers, once we let them know how much and little we've felt before. it's our best skill and nowhere more than Nevermore.

one day Ailsa will go there, because she has before. i hope it's not for a long time. our brief is to stay alive and, if we can, keep an eye out for others,

for those who care enough to see beauty
even though it's bad for us
to take too much
or suffer burden until the back breaks
and all hell comes with it

realty is reality
having shelter when the storm hits
is necessary and absolute
my house is my basic life

     Nevermore is actually *beauty*
    spelled back to itself
               quietly
     almost silently
like a melodic dream

in Nevermore, people don't know why they act the way they do.

24. *the shape of things*

there is energy to the man who sits by the bar dressed like he should be somewhere else, as he tries to clink bounce a 50p piece into a shot glass. at the far end, me, trying to work out the serial number on the receipt i have in my pocket and why it was given to me. i know they are testing me. i know one day i'll make it through to the afternoon of this long day. one day all the songs will fade the same way.

now, straightening up, nearly bouncing my head off the low ceiling, i take myself outside where the salt air is like a fine wine to be sniffed and tasted, to be savoured and to get drunk on.

esoteric life is a waste
and the way into any border is the shaky part;
like a needle laser, the way in is scary like childhood;
it's much scarier than most remember

i remember the tv not turning off –
the white dot that held the world
and my hands in bed as big as stone rocks
and the posters that eyes shone through
but once you're through the next part
the day is the same
but it looks different in the opal of your eye

i guess i'm like Ailsa, wishing the rest of the world could see the world as it really is. and then it hits me, like a happy laugh, that most do, once they reach a golden age, and even when things balance out again, they have that to rest awhile upon, like nesting birds who must watch their offspring fly.

and as i reach an old friend's door and push the button, on the other side of town a gentleman bounces a coin into a shot glass, heads up, and quits the bar.

there's a trio of children
and each is given a shape to place in their heads
one finds the shape fits round their thoughts like water
one finds the edges difficult and ugly but the detail dazzling
one finds the whole shape inside and out so beautiful, that they place it in their heart

25. beautiful mind

> still waters run deep
> waters run deep still
> run deep still waters
> deep still waters run
> time run beauty deep
> still
> waters
> time
> deep
> deep
> there is something beautiful
> about the way the mind orders

i wish you had seen
i believe we all do
it's lost in the conversations we have in Nevermore
lost to machismo and daily little talk
but sometimes
when drunk
it leaks out
and the place seems to hold it all in
inside wooden walls, or brick work late postmodern or such

i sometimes, sober, will pretend i'm still a child
and toe the line along the kerb
arms out
the child-like walk of a mind on Acid
and the way I've been since
has been blessed and cursed and all and all —
my Grandfather's parka
too big for me
great swinging arms

and the houses looked like they had just been built
and the paintwork fresh
and at night the green fake pastures –
so very, very green
almost glowed –
and the lights of the far-off peninsula
a lifetime times a thousand away

these are the days i remember
and cannot regret
for they explain the life to me
that half pokes round corners
and supresses giggles
when all life wants to do is guffaw and chortle
and drink in the sea air
and say, *come ahead*
the stars look as far as they actually are

and you my child, are blessed to see
blessed more to remember
blessed to be

26. *splinters*

★

i know where the thoughts go when there's nothing but breaks////i know it hurts me////lie
and feel the yolts like electracy through my head/my whole body yudders/////tv talked to me
earlier////////the bed feels like it's several feet before//////////////i'd drink wine.

★

there's a yawning gap to the day. the sludge of the sofa. the block i light and relight. the crumble
down. they don't like visits. i'm a charm of dark moods. i am not aware. i am not there. i say a
lyric to keep something. say it over and over into a mirror. it doesn't help.

★

the streets outside/////look, no, have black lines/the party upstairs sounds like hell//// sounds
like torture///one album keeps the mood swept back//////my whole being is back tinged///there
is something behind me////////at all times////i haven't slept in days/////i wall////////////////

★

arm becomes leg of chair | corner of room | batter corner ceiling | grey | becomes all | the fitting
| there are thousands behind me | they keep looking down | poking themselves forward | smiles |
all is calm | all is bright | but i'm half fighting |

this is neither pleasant or terrible, just is.

earlier i tried to get up and my body was a quarter the height of the door. upstairs the city streets
lay just below the landing. i have been here before. certain words drop out. worry about myself.
this is not happening now. this happened years ago. another time i climbed down a ladder into
blackness, came back up to find myself at a picnic table surrounded by heads and people under
them. on a barge, with laughter spinning in my ears. earlier i'd leapt in the starry water, still.
arguing which was better. talking and feeling like i'd written all their songs.
i am self.butwiththisiamsomehowsunhitsstarssameskyalltheoneha

★

pick

        butter

              yellow

                     light

    smile

                     arms

              body

        heart

alone

        foal

              scratch

                     red

    can't

                     stitching

              eyes

        steady

two

        sex

              soft

                     lips

    dumb

                     rocky

              whine

        wine

lines

        hi

              low

                     lies

stillest

it

matters

how

you

27. something for the lunch hour

<u>thesis</u>
value: 30
term: lambda
sex: ambi
course: north-northeast
property: silver
song: children's games
degree: 55
first is the worst, second is the best, third is the one with the wedding dress

<u>antithesis</u>
sex: neither
value: 1.618033988749894848204586834
term: phi
course: south-southwesterly
property: copper
song: popular
degree: 7
one two three four, won't you stay a little more?

<u>synthesis</u>
sex: both
value: 916
term: delta
course: all, magnetic north
property: bronze
song: classical
degree: 9
blue is just another form of white

28. the butterfly effect

white noise   a shape reaches out   time to make a leap
all those years   you were looking   believing
and believing   and lost   for all the good of it

instead   you
were here   all long
all it took was   that bar where
i thought everyone   has their northern cross
to bear and the air circles   the centre of the room and
the butterfly lecture clicked in one from years ago and the centre
was no longer me they said never open brollies indoors but once
done there's little in it we put too much store in the hidden
in the end it's so simple and easily done white noise the
difference is i can see how many more need help how
many more
i can reach with a hand as easily as they helped me
just remember there is no centre but the void is a
smile because you place it there before the door
closes and the   world nods and
moves   along

i told the policeman, eyes wet with tears, i just wanted to move the world on a little bit. he said *they don't have an issue with you, just don't go that way again.* his name was Peter. i took the hint.

29. at least

the one word
i regret if regret is a word
is 'pointless'

said that time
in the hour of a physical test
earphones in hand
Great-Grandfather pulled from the grave
(i have to be called down to this?)
it became a medal in the hand
to throw down at the bar
orange-lit-polished wood
that one cursed word

and the next so-many months were not the same
because the strength, or break, in a word
is in its meaning in another's ear

i thought i'd sorted someone home
found a lost grave
but lost myself instead

      sing a song of sixpence

but what i did was

      sing a song of sixpence

but what i did was

      sing a song of sixpence

rattle of skin – the roundabout – the circle – the millstone –

at least you performed
there's no time like the present
be good, if you can't be good…
we all use each other
at least you came home
you know about the dreamtime and the inside of your head
knock 'em dead

30. *what lets the light in*

what have i learned?

there's no *one* for anyone
not a person
but many

there was a time
when my backyard
was the Garden of Gethsemane
and it was all mapped out

what i did had to be perfect
everything perfect
it is finished and all that
and there are many different ways out
there is more than one door

the doors are just woodland desire lines
and the soul doesn't see the streets

this is just my version of truth
the only thing i can boast
is that i'm still here to say it
i don't know whether it's worth walking through the mind
but friends tell me (in their own ways)
it's better to know yourself
i just wish it didn't cost so much

every time you open yourself up
he told me they'd strip me of every level of sin

random doesn't happen
how random is random?
the hand on the tiller knows magnetic north
because it's hard wired in the skin
a life lived in metaphor
has to be let go sometimes
you risk your life every time you swim
every time you cross the road
kick the kerb

answer 2

help
is a diamond
light that breaks the
skin as it enters in. help is the
answer to every prayer even those
of thanksgiving and wary is the breath that
asks. help turns itself out. it finds succour most in those
who help others after themselves. this is the key, and the key is
always obvious as it cuts its edge into your skin but often goes unnoticed
as your mind fumbles over thoughts like the contents of a pocket
of air. throw everything at a friend, see what lands like paper
planes skidding across pub and café tables. you
meet all sorts in this line of work. the
heart may feel like it takes
place on one side of
the body, it's
both.

the best and worst come together in tryptic, like the call in the night. you shudder, your hand to the phone in the quickness of it, the thoughts chasing the shadows round the room. third time this week. too many for such a young head on aching shoulders. but if it weren't for these, would we still become the people we wished to be, still with a part missing? the final baulk never quite fits but we take all of them and place them in our hearts. but yes i have to leave the answer unsaid because to try and express it, well, that's like changing the world i guess. it doesn't knead you shouldn't try, it doesn't meal, you shuddern't tri, it doesn't mean you shouldn't try.
this is just a fragment. the answer is not only personal, it's there to invite you to walk further, and to keep walking. at least, this is my truth. carved it on my arm once. you should try it. joke.

31. *when you draw the many edges together*

deadline loomed like air looms
for bedlam's best & finest
we all know how time slacks
and then snaps tight

woollen socks   bless them all
another space cadet   wound up

the sound of the radio told me
this performance will change everything

the white sheet – they will tie you up in and cut you – you will live forever

there is only one book
written over and over
you are its villain
you shouldn't have looked

lighten up, it's a comedy

no one runs faster than Achilles

i had them in stitches round hands of poker
playing through part of the night
there's always humour in our humors

murmur of the heart
i love this world
even as it feels so angry and hard-tongued
in the sadness on the tv screen

let me be a kid this once
and wave at trucks as they pass
because they know i know you know
and you know the pleasure that brings

even with my head in my hands
shaking with the sound of the tv eating into the air
i bear no anger
i love whatever will be
and love is a slack tongue word when i'm here
because my tongue feels tightened
by the pain that shouts from the walls –
tell a joke to keep the heat in

and what have i answered?

fifteen years spent trying
with some blue-fingered map
that maps my hand
that maps my footsteps
and cries my tears
that i may have answered a little
at a price, all heavily told
but i have learned so much instead:
to have, to give, to hold

now, now
there, there

living by the familiar oneness of the ocean
it starts to snow
a marker of my Grandfather saying *hello*
i can still feel the warmth of a high feeling
as long as i don't get too exposed to the winter sun

that shines like a disc
but today is just cold knitted into bare fingers
and January – a different January
lays out halfway through

a friend comes bustling through the café door
to ask and to tell, a smile i always find kindest
amidst the bluster that she does so boldly

i'll try and sum
up before we move along; much of what
i believed is left in boxes in an attic over a room
changed by age – it looks younger now. the attic still
remains the same: the great hulk of shadowy things, a doll's
house. they still call you know. when i was young i believed in
animals yet unfound and lamented those no longer here; now
i am older i believe, sometimes, in stranger things all done by
spirits and men, and there's little difference between now
and then apart from the harm i can do to myself.
maybe they aren't so different; maybe age
is just the brain's way of readying us
for an ending.

ACKNOWLEDGEMENTS

With thanks to Eyewear Publishing – Todd Swift, Cate Myddleton-Evans, Edwin Smet.

TITLES INCLUDE

EYEWEAR
POETRY

ELSPETH SMITH DANGEROUS CAKES
CALEB KLACES BOTTLED AIR
GEORGE ELLIOTT CLARKE ILLICIT SONNETS
BARBARA MARSH TO THE BONEYARD
DON SHARE UNION
SHEILA HILLIER HOTEL MOONMILK
SJ FOWLER THE ROTTWEILER'S GUIDE TO THE DOG OWNER
JEMMA BORG THE ILLUMINATED WORLD
KEIRAN GODDARD FOR THE CHORUS
COLETTE SENSIER SKINLESS
ANDREW SHIELDS THOMAS HARDY LISTENS TO LOUIS ARMSTRONG
JAN OWEN THE OFFHAND ANGEL
SEAN SINGER HONEY & SMOKE
HESTER KNIBBE HUNGERPOTS
MEL PRYOR SMALL NUCLEAR FAMILY
TONY CHAN FOUR POINTS FOURTEEN LINES
MARIA APICHELLA PSALMODY
ALICE ANDERSON THE WATERMARK
BEN PARKER THE AMAZING LOST MAN
MARION MCCREADY MADAME ECOSSE
MARIELA GRIFFOR DECLASSIFIED
MARK YAKICH THE DANGEROUS BOOK OF POETRY FOR PLANES
HASSAN MELEHY A MODEST APOCALYPSE
KATE NOAKES PARIS, STAGE LEFT
U.S. DHUGA THE SIGHT OF A GOOSE GOING BAREFOOT
TERENCE TILLER THE COLLECTED POEMS
MATTHEW STEWART THE KNIVES OF VILLALEJO
PAUL MULDOON SADIE AND THE SADISTS
JENNA CLAKE FORTUNE COOKIE
TARA SKURTU THE AMOEBA GAME
MANDY KAHN GLENN GOULD'S CHAIR
CAL FREEMAN FIGHT SONGS
TIM DOOLEY WEEMOED
MATTHEW PAUL THE EVENING ENTERTAINMENT
NIALL BOURKE DID YOU PUT THE WEASELS OUT?
USHA KISHORE IMMIGRANT
LEAH UMANSKY THE BARBAROUS CENTURY
STEVE KRONEN HOMAGE TO MISTRESS OPPENHEIMER
FAISAL MOHYUDDIN THE DISPLACED CHILDREN OF DISPLACED CHILDREN
ALEX HOUEN RING CYCLE
COLIN DARDIS THE X OF Y
JAMES FINNEGAN HALF-OPEN DOOR
SOHINI BASAK WE LIVE IN THE NEWNESS OF SMALL DIFFERENCES
MICHAEL WILSON BEDLAM'S BEST & FINEST
GALE BURNS MUTE HOUSE
REBECCA CLOSE VALID, VIRTUAL, VEGETABLE REALITY
KEN EVANS TRUE FORENSICS
ALEX WYLIE SECULAR GAMES